INSIDE SPECIAL FORCES ™

SPECIAL OPS:
WEAPONS AND GEAR

David Kassnoff

rosen publishing's
rosen central

New York

Published in 2015 by The Rosen Publishing Group, Inc.
29 East 21st Street, New York, NY 10010

Copyright © 2015 by The Rosen Publishing Group, Inc.

First Edition

Library of Congress Cataloging-in-Publication Data

Kassnoff, David.
Special ops: weapons and gear/David Kassnoff.—First edition.
     pages cm.—(Inside special forces)
Includes bibliographical references and index.
ISBN 978-1-4777-7567-7 (library bound)—ISBN 978-1-4777-7569-1 (pbk.)—
ISBN 978-1-4777-7570-7 (6-pack)
1. Special forces (Military science)—United States—Equipment and supplies—Juvenile literature. 2. Military weapons—United States—Juvenile literature. I. Title.
UA34.S64K37 2014
356'.160284—dc23

2014021204

Manufactured in Malaysia

CONTENTS

It's hot. It's cold. It's wet. It's dark. The pack is incredibly heavy with gear. Weapons and ammunition weigh a ton. And the mission's just begun. Welcome to Special Forces.

The role of soldiers serving in Special Forces in the U.S. armed forces has changed in recent years. So have their weapons and equipment. Following the attacks of September 11, 2001, U.S. military troops fought long and complicated wars in Iraq and Afghanistan. Combating terrorism, the Taliban, and Al Qaeda terrorist groups became important roles for Special Forces in the region. So did helping leaders of Iraq and Afghanistan govern themselves.

Movies and television often show Special Forces operating in harsh conditions or on secret missions to capture and eliminate terrorists. Special Forces missions often require soldiers to train for extended, intense combat and noncombat duty. They must learn to use a range of specialized equipment, from weapons to vehicles to survival gear.

Beyond Iraq and Afghanistan, Special Operations ("Special Ops") servicemen serve in Korea, Somalia, Vietnam, North America, and elsewhere. The U.S. Special Operations Command is headquartered at McDill Air Force Base in Florida. It oversees training, missions, and deployment of some sixty-six thousand servicemen and servicewomen worldwide.

Special Forces is part of the U.S. Special Operations Command, or USSOCOM. Its mission is to provide fully capable Special Operations forces to defend the United States and its interests and to coordinate global operations against terrorist networks. This means USSOCOM forces take part in civil affairs (working with local foreign leaders), counterinsurgency and counterterrorism, searching for weapons of mass destruction, foreign internal

A nighttime mission called for these U.S. Army Rangers to rely on night-vision devices—as well as a multipurpose canine—to pursue their targets.

5

defense, hostage rescue and recovery, security force assistance, preparing a region for military missions, combat support, reconnaissance, unconventional warfare, and more.

To accomplish their missions, Special Ops forces use gear and weapons that reflect advances in technology and changes in their assignments. These include advanced night vision devices and high-tech body armor. Rifles, handguns, helmets, and vehicles are essential gear.

A Special Forces warrior in theater may carry a pack of essential gear weighing 65 pounds (29 kilograms) or more. This is about the weight of a bag of concrete mix. Special Ops soldiers carry a lot of gear. For example, an Army Ranger's kit will include body armor, pouches for magazines of ammunition, hydration, grenades, and an individual deployment kit that contains multiple tools for maintaining weapons, cutting through straps, probing for land mines, and other important tasks. That heavy pack also includes a sub-belt for survival gear, MREs (meals, ready to eat), and other essentials.

The list of today's weapons and gear is long. Let's roll.

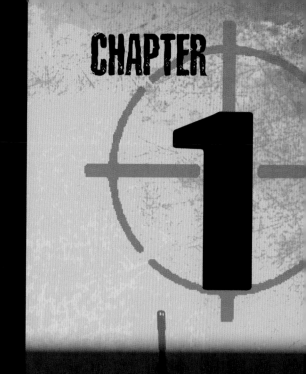

LOCK AND LOAD: SOF FIREARMS

When Special Operations Forces (SOF) operatives deploy to direct combat missions, they carry several types of firearms, ranging from semiautomatic pistols to powerful rifles and machine guns. Here, we'll take a look at some of those weapons.

M4 CARBINE: THE WORKHORSE RIFLE

The M4 carbine rifle is the workhorse of today's U.S. armed forces, having seen duty in most recent Middle East conflicts. The M4 weighs about 7.5 pounds (3.4 kg) when loaded with a single magazine of thirty rounds. It has a maximum effective range of about one-third of a mile (500–600 meters). The M4 fires a .223-caliber round. It can shoot twelve to fifteen rounds per minute at a sustained rate of fire. Soldiers can also select semiautomatic firing and three-round bursts. The M4A1 version offers fully automatic firing.

The M4 includes a collapsible stock, a flat-top upper receiver rail to mount a sight or scope, and a detachable handle/rear aperture site assembly. Extended, accurate range is why soldiers use the M4 rifle. This weapon shoots farther, even in close quarters. Using the M4, a soldier operating in close quarters can engage targets at extended range with accurate, lethal fire. The Army Rangers add several

The M4 carbine shown here offers soldiers impressive extended range, even in close-quarter missions in alleyways and narrow streets.

modifications to the M4, including an EO Tech 553 holographic reflex sight, LA-5 infrared laser, sound suppressor, fore grip, and M3X visible tactical light. These are parts of a special modifications kit developed by USSOCOM. These accessories help a soldier aim at his target in fog or at night.

Other add-ons include a quick-release M203 grenade launcher that, when mounted below the M4's barrel, gives the weapon additional firepower. Using a single 40-millimeter ammunition cartridge, the M203 can effectively blow open doors and bunkers. It can even disable nonarmored vehicles. Soldiers can add a night-vision device, known as the AN/PVS-4, to help target enemies in darkness.

Sales of select-fire and fully automatic rifles such as the M4 are limited to the military and police agencies. Civilians cannot own these rifles, but replica weapons modified to resemble and perform similarly to shortened M4 rifles are sold to the public.

M16 CARBINE

The M4 is based on an older version of the M16 than the one currently in use. The M16A4 assault rifle traces its design to the long-lived AR-15 assault rifle. The M16A4 is used by the Marine Corps and select U.S. Army units. It's slightly heavier than the M4. It also has a longer effective range. While most U.S. SOF rely on the smaller M4 or M4A1, the USMC Fleet Antiterrorism Security Teams and the Marine Special Operations Support Group (MSOSG) use the M16A4.

WOMEN SERVING IN SPECIAL FORCES

In June 2013, officials at the U.S. Pentagon took steps to allow women to begin training as Army Rangers by July 2015 and as Navy SEALs by March 2016. The Pentagon briefed congressional leaders, telling them that male and female service members would need to meet the same physical and mental requirements in order to qualify for "front-line" deployment in infantry, armor, and commando duty across the services. Defense Secretary Chuck Hagel directed the services to move forward with their plans. The decision to open these elite units to women was ordered by Hagel's predecessor, Leon Panetta.

M240B: CONTINUOUS FIREPOWER

For greater firepower and range, the U.S. Marines and Army use the M240B (B for "Bravo") machine gun. This heavy automatic weapon provides a continuous high rate of fire to attack long-range targets. Rounds are fed into the machine gun via a disintegrating belt, giving soldiers a nonstop source of fire. Using a 7.62mm round, the M240 can fire one hundred rounds per minute in sustained fire. In rapid-fire situations it can fire two hundred rounds per minute. However, because of the high heat created in rapid-fire use, the M240's barrel must be changed every two minutes. In short, rapid bursts, the weapon can fire 650–950 rounds per minute.

The M240 is not an easy weapon to carry. With its permanent bipod legs attached to the barrel, the machine gun weighs 24 pounds (10.8 kg). This is more than three times heavier than the M4 carbine. When mounted on a tripod or a vehicle mount for stability, the M240 delivers a range of 1.1 miles to 2.31 miles (1.77–3.71 kilometers). It can also be mounted on tanks or light armored vehicles. In Special Forces operations, it may be mounted near the rear of Ground Mobility Vehicles (GMV) in convoys.

M240 machine guns (above) are often mounted on Ground Mobility Vehicles. They deliver continuous firepower and a range of greater than 2 miles (3.2 km).

While the M240B is a heavy weapon, it can be hand-carried and fired when necessary. It can be fitted with additional sights and devices to help soldiers aim and fire with precision. These include the M145 sight and an AN/PEQ-2 illuminating laser sight.

PISTOLS: COMPACT FIREPOWER

In Special Forces missions, pistols usually serve as defensive weapons in close-range situations. Their smaller rounds don't travel nearly as far as rounds fired from a rifle. Adopted by the U.S. military in 1985, the M9 pistol is a semiautomatic, double-action pistol. It has a rail system beneath the barrel, where a soldier can attach an Integrated Laser White Light Pointer (ILWLP). The ILWLP helps the soldier aim more accurately, providing a tactical advantage in close combat operations. This addition (which became available with the rail system on the M9A1 version in 2006) has resulted in increased lethality and survivability for Special Forces soldiers.

In the marines and army, the M9 is the standard sidearm. Firing a 9 mm round, the M9 is designed for closer encounters with targets. It has a range of about 55 yards (50 m). This is half the length of a football field. The M9 Beretta weighs about 2.5 pounds (1.1 kg). Its magazine holds 15 NATO standard rounds. It uses a double-action trigger, in which the hammer can be cocked and fired by the single pull of the trigger. The M9 is carried in a holster. The M9 is the military version of Beretta's 92F semiautomatic pistol that civilians may buy.

While the M9 Beretta is issued to most Navy personnel, the U.S. Navy adopted a different sidearm for its Navy SEALs in 1986, choosing the SIG Sauer P226. The SIG Sauer M11 (or P228), a smaller version of the P226 using a thirteen-round magazine, was adopted by the Navy SEALs in 1989. Currently in use today, the SIG Sauer P226 Mark 25 uses a fifteen-round magazine of 9mm bullets. It can also fire .40-caliber S&W rounds or .357-caliber SIG rounds.

U.S. Army forces use M9 Berettas at a practice range in Afghanistan. The U.S. military began using the M9 in 1985.

PISTOLS FOR FUND-RAISING?

Gun collecting is a centuries-old hobby and business. It can also be a way to help those in need. In 2004, SIGARMS of Exeter, New Hampshire, created a limited edition of special SIG Sauer P226 pistols produced to the exact same specifications as those used by Navy SEALs since 1986. Designated SIG P226-9-NAVY, this version included a corrosion-resistant finish on internal parts, contrast sights, a slide engraved with an anchor to designate it as a Naval Special Warfare pistol, and a unique serial number.

Sales of these NSW-engraved pistols helped raise more than $100,000 for the Special Operations Warrior Foundation. The foundation provides support, primarily scholarships, so that the children of Special Operations personnel who have died serving their country will be able to attend college. Learn more at http://www.specialops.org.

The U.S. Marines Special Operations Command (MARSOC) likes the M45 close quarter battle pistol, modified to meet its own requirements. Until Colt Defense received a 2013 contract to build new M45 pistols, gunsmiths at the Marine Corps' Precision Weapon Section created hand-refurbished versions of the M1911 with ranges of up to 164 feet (50 m). The standard magazine holds seven or eight .45-caliber rounds. The loaded weapon weighs about 2.5 pounds (1.1 kg).

CHAPTER 2

WEAPONRY OF THE GREEN BERETS

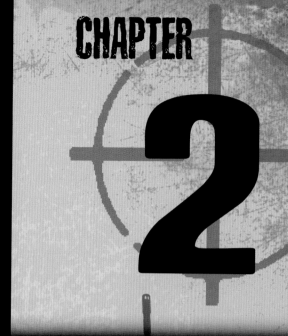

In the U.S. Army, Special Forces units (Green Berets) perform seven missions: unconventional warfare, foreign internal defense, special reconnaissance, direct action, combating terrorism, counter-proliferation, and information operations. Their missions can include rescuing hostages, performing humanitarian service, gathering and providing information, and counter-proliferation, which is fighting to prevent the sale and distribution of weapons to terrorists and potential enemies of the United States. Created in 1952, the Green Berets' motto is *De Oppress Liber*, or "to Free the Oppressed." While other elite military units (including Navy SEALs and Army Rangers) are called Special Operations Forces, only the Green Berets have the official designation as U.S. Army Special Forces.

The training to become a Green Beret is demanding. It goes far beyond the basic training army-enlisted men and women receive. Candidates are trained to survive in harsh environments and become advanced marksmen. They learn how to navigate across difficult terrain, escape capture, speak other languages, and serve in airborne duty.

The gear Army Special Forces use builds upon the weapons shared by other branches of the service: the M4 and M16 rifle, the M9 Beretta pistol, and the M240B machine gun. For specialized missions, the

A U.S. Army Special Forces soldier carries an M4 rifle and wears body armor alongside an Iraqi soldier in Diwaniyah, Iraq.

Green Berets rely on specialized gear. For example, a Special Forces weapons sergeant must be skilled in operating a variety of weapons, including those used by allies and enemies.

HEAVY WEAPONS IN THEATER

U.S. heavy weapons include the 4.2-inch (10.7-centimeter) and 120mm mortars and the M40 106mm recoilless rifle. The M40 is a breech-loaded, 439-pound (199-kg), single-shot, crew-served recoilless rifle. The M40 can be used in both antitank and antipersonnel roles. It can fire artillery-type shells. The M120 120mm mortar, smaller than a field artillery gun, is usually transported by a trailer attached to a High Mobility Multipurpose Wheeled Vehicle (HMMWV or Humvee). It fires fin-stabilized ammunition—essentially, small rocket-like projectiles—from a smooth bore.

Special Forces soldiers also carry grenades, but these aren't the pineapple-style grenades from World War II movies. Troops use some hand-thrown grenades, but other grenades are fired with a high-explosive charge from single-shot or automatic grenade launchers with a caliber of 30 mm or 40 mm. This launches an egg-shaped grenade up to about 1 1/3 miles (2,200 meters). Grenade launchers include:

- The M79 grenade launcher, a break-open weapon that fires single-shot 40mm rounds. It can be carried on the shoulder and fired like a rifle. (It is also used by Navy SEALs.)

- The M32 multishot grenade launcher, a handheld, semiautomatic, revolving action launcher that can be loaded with six 40mm rounds. It resembles a short rifle with a large revolving magazine in between the trigger and barrel.
- The M203 grenade launcher, which can be fitted to the M16A4 rifle and the M4 carbine with a quick-attach bracket and a leaf sight.
- The MK47 grenade launcher, also known as the Advanced Lightweight Grenade Launcher (ALGL) system. It's a reliable, portable 40mm grenade

This U.S. Marine corporal demonstrates an M203 multishot grenade launcher, attached to an M4 carbine, during a training exercise at Clark Field in the Philippines.

weapon system suited for mobile, tactical combat soldier units. Often fired from a seated position, the 40-pound (18-kg) MK47 is used by many Special Operations units as a replacement for the older MK19 grenade launcher. The MK47 acts like a giant revolver, using a rotating cylinder inside that rotates

DON'T BRING A GUN TO A KNIFE FIGHT

Is there a special knife used by the Green Berets? The most familiar is the M9 bayonet, in use since the mid-1980s. But a number of knife manufacturers offer comparable products to the armed forces. Which ones are used becomes a matter of choice for soldiers because a knife is more of a survival tool than a defensive or offensive tool.

A 7-inch (18-cm) KA-BAR steel knife is issued to army soldiers. It is also used by navy servicemen and marines. The army began issuing the ASEK survival knife with a 5-inch (13-cm) blade to servicemen in 2003. The Yarborough knife by Chris Reeve Knives of Idaho—also sold to civilians as the Green Beret Knife—features a 7-inch (18-cm) stainless steel blade. It is issued to Special Forces soldiers upon graduation from their challenging training. However, many soldiers view it as a symbol of their achievement and store it safely while purchasing a more practical knife for use in the field.

each 40mm round into firing position. It can fire up to three hundred rounds per minute.

What is today's hand-thrown grenade of choice? The M67 fragmentation hand grenade can kill enemies within a 15-foot (5-m) radius and injure those within a radius of 45 feet (15 m). The M67 is a small, round sphere weighing 14 ounces (397 grams), filled with 6.5 ounces (184 g) of high explosive. A soldier can throw this grenade about 40 yards (37 m).

A U.S. Marine fires an M136 AT4 light antiarmor weapon during training. The M136 is considered a primary light antitank weapon.

The M67 grenade will send fragments of scorching metal as far as 250 feet (76 m). But those fragments, while deadly, don't do as much damage as the rapid expansion of air pressure when the grenade explodes. While an adversary might be able to duck the explosion, when a grenade explodes, it triggers a rapid compression of air through an enemy's ears that can cause instantaneous brain damage, incapacitation, or death to the victim.

TANK KILLERS

Need to disable a tank and its crew? Portable anti-tank weapons can take out an armored vehicle. The M136 AT4 is the army's main light antitank weapon. Like the M40, it's a recoilless rifle soldiers use to defeat armored threats. Resembling a compact bazooka, the shoulder-fired M136 packs a powerful punch: an 84mm high-explosive, rocket-type anti-tank warhead that can penetrate the skin of armored vehicles up to 400 mm—that's 15.7 inches—thick. The 15-pound (6.8 kg) M136 has an effective range of up to 985 feet (or about 250–300 m).

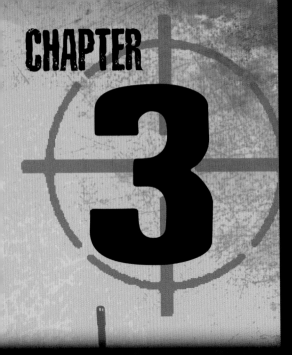

CHAPTER 3

THE GEAR OF SPECIAL FORCES SERGEANTS

Special Forces sergeants serve in a variety of functions. Engineers, medics, and communications sergeants each play an essential role in a twelve-person team known as an operational detachment alpha, or an A-team.

Special Forces engineer sergeants are specialists in many tasks, from demolitions and the construction of field fortifications to topographic survey techniques. They rely on explosive devices, surveying instruments, and basic construction equipment to perform their jobs. They are as expert with power tools, hammers, bolt cutters, and electrical wiring as they are with Composition C-4 moldable explosives, detonators, and blasting caps. Special Forces engineer sergeants are also required to be qualified divers, swimmers, parachutists, and endurance runners.

High altitude low opening (HALO) parachute jumps are an important military tactic. Here, a U.S. Army sergeant repacks a parachute between training jumps.

CELL PHONES DON'T WORK HERE

In most combat zones, few cell towers or telephone wires dot the rugged landscape. So, the role of a Special Forces communications sergeant is critical. These communication experts operate every kind of communications gear, from encrypted satellite radio systems to old-style, high-frequency Morse code key systems. Like engineer sergeants, they often reach their mission objectives via parachute, land, or water and may be asked to detonate or deactivate explosives.

Now in deployment is the AN/PRC-148 Multiband Inter/Intra Team Radio (MBITR). Both Special Operations Command (SOCOM) units and other U.S. forces use this hand-held, secure, digital radio. Its range is about 12 miles (19 km). It can be attached to a soldier's headset and is used for voice and data communications. Developed by SOCOM and Thales Communications, MBITRs are widely used by U.S. Special Operations Forces units.

Other equipment Special Forces communications sergeants use can include:

• Wideband tactical radios, which USSOCOM forces can use to send and receive tactical voice, video, and data communications. They are used in surveillance, assessing situations, and in reconnaissance combat situations. They bring Internet-like communications to the battlefield.

• Handheld multiband tactical radios that can provide Special Forces and army soldiers with

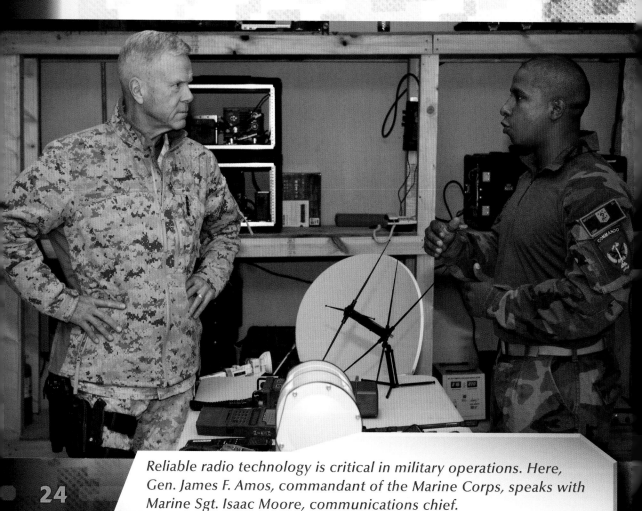

Reliable radio technology is critical in military operations. Here, Gen. James F. Amos, commandant of the Marine Corps, speaks with Marine Sgt. Isaac Moore, communications chief.

wideband networking capabilities, as well as line-of-sight, ground-to-air, and tactical satellite voice and data communications.

- Situational awareness video receivers (SAVR) that can transmit ISR (intelligence, surveillance, and reconnaissance) video feeds directly to ground forces, showing them what an aircraft or unmanned aerial vehicle is viewing in real time.
- Satellite phones that send radio signals to a satellite in orbit, which then resends a signal back to Earth. The signal is then routed to the Public Switched Telephone Network, where the receiver can connect to the caller. Satellite phones can be used in remote areas where no cellular towers exist.
- Vehicle intercom systems that allow soldiers to share in-vehicle voice and data communication, tactical network connectivity, and battle management system among crew members.
- Ruggedized computers and tablets that soldiers use to connect to wideband networks to share photos and files, receive full-motion video feeds from unmanned drones, and remotely control tactical radios.

TREATING WOUNDED SOLDIERS

Medical sergeants on Special Forces teams deal with first aid and first response medical emergencies when soldiers or civilians are injured. Known as "18Ds," they are trained to deal with trauma situations—severe, life-threatening cases. They also have a working knowledge of dentistry, veterinary care, public sanitation, water quality, and optometry. They cannot carry all the gear found in a civilian or military hospital. However, they do carry masks, rubber gloves, first-aid kits, dressings for soldiers' wounds, and pharmacology packs with drugs to block pain or antibiotics to help control infection.

Most army soldiers carry a custom-designed first-aid kit, newly issued in 2013. The original individual first aid dit (IFAK) contained a combat application

MEDICINE FROM ABOVE AND ON THE GROUND

Noncommissioned officers in Special Operations Forces are trained to use equipment and techniques used only by medical professionals in conventional forces. Often, these medics rely on medical equipment that is dropped in containers by parachute to diagnose and treat their patients. These "care packages" can include broad-spectrum antibiotics, narcotics, and fluid administration kits, which not all conventional medics carry. Portable ultrasound devices are used to look for internal bleeding.

The real surprise? Sometimes, Special Operations medical sergeants are just high-school graduates. But in the field, during battle conditions, they can find themselves performing the work of an experienced doctor.

tourniquet, an elastic bandage kit, bandage gauze, surgical adhesive tape, a nasopharyngeal airway tube to assist a victim in breathing, and patient exam gloves. The new IFAK II kit added a second tourniquet, a tactical combat casualty card to document the first aid a soldier receives, a marker, an eye shield, a rubber seal with a valve for sucking chest wounds, and a strap cutter. This new kit helps soldiers deal with immediate point-of-injury care until a medical sergeant can assess and treat the injuries.

SOCOM relies on two types of military medics: Special Forces medical sergeants (designated 18Ds) and Special Operations combat medics (SOCMs). SOCMs are assigned to the 160th Special Operations Aviation Regiment (Airborne) and Special Operations Support Command (Airborne). The 18Ds are cross-trained members of the Special Forces (Green Beret) alpha teams. About 80 percent of SOCOM medics are 18Ds.

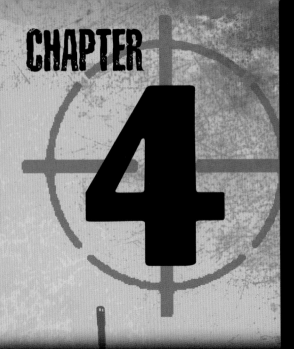

CHAPTER 4

OUTFITTING THE NAVY SEALS

The Navy SEALs are the best known of the U.S. Naval Special Operation Forces. "SEAL" comes from "Sea, Air, Land," the three environments in which these elite teams operate. Each team is a multipurpose combat force, trained to conduct a variety of Special Operations missions in all environments. A SEAL Team is the heart of the Naval Special Warfare force.

SEALs conduct clandestine, or secret, missions. They infiltrate areas by fixed-wing aircraft (planes), rotary-wing aircraft (helicopters), navy surface ships, combatant craft, submarines, and ground vehicles. They are supported by special warfare combatant-craft crewmen on vessels and vehicles. Enablers (technicians) provide SEAL teams with mobile communications, tactical code-breaking support, and bomb disposal services.

Because they are deployed to many different missions, including direct action, counterinsurgency, and counterterrorism activities, Navy SEALs use an astonishing array of equipment. However, many of their high-tech devices are confidential for security reasons. The best-known recent SEAL team mission involved the latest weapons and technology, and it was televised to a very small live audience.

NAVY SEAL TEAM 6 IN ACTION

On May 2, 2011, Navy SEALs descended from stealth-equipped helicopters into a darkened, walled compound in Abbottabad, Pakistan. Within minutes, they had captured and killed international terrorist Osama bin

The navy's parachute demonstration team is called the Leap Frogs. Its members include U.S. Navy SEALs, including the two special warfare operators first class shown here.

THE WEAPON WITH FOUR LEGS

When Navy SEAL Team 6 stormed Osama bin Laden's compound in Pakistan in 2011, the force consisted of seventy-nine men and one dog. The dog wore a special earpiece so his master could command him via radio. While the breed of the specially trained dog wasn't disclosed, the *New York Times* speculated that it was either a German shepherd or a Belgian Malinois. Both breeds are skilled at tracking people in hiding.

Some six hundred dogs took part in operations during the U.S. military's work in Afghanistan and Iraq. Used widely in Special Operations, dogs can locate explosive devices more quickly than humans. They also sniff out booby-trapped doorways, patrol secure areas, sky-dive from altitudes of 25,000 feet (7.6 km), and helocast, or jump with soldiers from a hovering helicopter into water. SEAL-trained Belgian Malinois are trained to attack adversaries carrying firearms. A German shepherd or Malinois can subdue a human foe because the dog runs twice as fast.

How important is the role of dogs in Special Operations? In 2009, a dog named Remco was awarded a posthumous Silver Star after he charged an insurgent's hideout in Afghanistan. The Silver Star is one of the navy's highest honors.

Laden, architect of the September 11, 2001, attacks on the World Trade Center, the Pentagon, and other potential targets.

That day made Navy SEAL Team 6 world famous. However, aside from one team member who wrote a book under the pseudonym Mark Owen, the team's members remain unknown. TV viewers did see photos of President Barack Obama and other top officials watching events unfold on a video monitor. The classified video of the May 2 raid didn't just materialize in the White House control center. It was captured with digital video and transmitted via satellite signals.

SEAL TEAM RIFLES

SEAL teams have access to the most advanced weapons, including the FN MK20 MOD 0 Sniper Support Rifle, the most current version of the MK17 Combat Support Rifle. This weapon is one of several Special Operations Forces Combat assault rifles that were designed as a modular "family" of SCAR weapons. SEAL teams also use the FN SCAR STD assault rifle, which has a 16-inch (41-cm) barrel and takes 7.62mm NATO caliber rounds. A Navy SEAL can switch to a shorter 13-inch (33-cm) barrel for close-quarter combat in about five minutes. The rifle is then called SCAR-H (for "Heavy") CQC. The soldier can add an FN40 grenade launcher to the lower rail of the rifle, beneath the barrel, for more firepower. Navy SEALs also have access to the AK-47 assault rifle. AK-47s are known for reliability and water resistance, making them a good fit for Navy SEALs missions.

MACHINE GUNS TO PISTOLS

Navy SEALs use several semiautomatic and automatic machine guns. The M14 7.62 semiautomatic machine gun fires a 7.62mm round from a 20-round magazine as far as 800 yards (731.5 m). The gas-operated, air-cooled M249 5.56mm machine gun provides a quick-change barrel that gunners can swap out to help prevent jams or overheating. The M240B/N (also called the M60) machine gun is also used.

The HK MP5N is a "machine pistol" and fires a 9mm round. It can fire up to 800 rounds per minute from a detachable magazine box containing 15 or 30 rounds. The weapon features an ambidextrous trigger system with positions for safe, single fire and full automatic fire, plus a threaded barrel. Unloaded, the HK MP5N weighs 5.5 pounds (2.5 kg). Its range is about 200 meters, or 219 yards. The MP5SD version includes an aluminum or wet-technology steel sound suppressor.

The HK MK23 was developed at the request of USSOCOM for use by elite military units, including the Navy SEALs and the Army Special Forces. (HK stands for Heckler & Koch, the gun's manufacturer.) It's a .45 caliber semiautomatic pistol that can be outfitted with a laser aiming module and a sound suppressor. The Smith & Wesson 686 .357 revolver may look old-fashioned, but it can fire its seven rounds either in or out of the water.

The M60 machine gun (also called the M240B/N) features a barrel-mounted bi-pod for stability. It first saw action in 1957.

HEAVIER WEAPONS

The FN Mk 13 grenade launcher weighs about 6 pounds (2.7 kg), includes a leaf sight, and fires 40mm grenades. Its retractable stock makes it easy to transport and set up. It attaches to a SCAR rifle and is fired with a separate trigger.

The light antitank weapons the SEALs use include the 25-pound (11.3-kg) MAAW M3 (Multi-Role Anti-Armor/Anti-Personnel Weapon System), an 84mm shoulder-fired, recoilless antiarmor and antipersonnel weapon. The M72 LAW is a shoulder-fired, light antitank rocket that can pierce through armor that is 12 inches (30 cm) thick. It has an effective range of up to 720 feet (220 m).

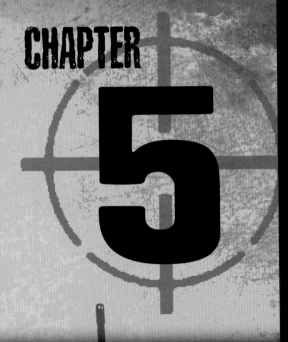

CHAPTER 5

BY AIR, LAND, AND WATER

How do Special Operations Forces travel on land, on the water, and in the air? Each military branch plays a part in Special Forces deployment. The Air Force Special Operations Command includes combat controllers, pararescue men, special operations weathermen, tactical air control parties, aviators, and combat aviation advisors. Their roles are to serve as combat-ready Air Force Special Operations Forces to conduct and support global special operations missions. Their gear include a variety of fixed-wing and rotary-wing aircraft.

Experts believe SEAL Team 6 flew into Abbottabad in May 2011 aboard MH-60 Black Hawk helicopters that had been heavily shielded with stealth technology panels. The stealth coverings helped the aircraft evade radar detection. No public photos of these helicopters exist. But one "helo" crashed in bin Laden's compound, leaving fragments for Pakistani experts to examine.

Vehicles play an important role in Special Operations missions. In addition to transporting the forces, they can be equipped with mounted weapons that troops use to repel attackers or strike at targets. Here's a look at some of the helicopters, surface vehicles, and watercraft these forces use.

HELICOPTERS FOR TRANSPORT AND ASSAULT

The MH-6M Little Bird transports up to six combat troops. It is flown by a crew of two. Its top speed is 143 miles per hour (230 kilometers per hour), and its range is 230 nautical miles (265 miles, or 426 km). Army Special Forces and other departments use this highly maneuverable light helicopter, both for utility and attack missions.

The workhorses of Special Operations missions are the MH-60K/L/M Black Hawk and the MH-60L/M Black Hawk Defensive Armed Penetrator (the "K/L/M" and the "L/M" indicate newer and older variants of the helicopters). MH-60 helos provide armed escort and fire support for Special Operations Forces. An MH-60 has two turboshaft engines, a top speed of 222 miles per hour (357 km/h), and a range of 450 nautical miles (518 miles, or 833 km). It will cruise at 138 miles per hour (222 km/h) and can be refueled in flight. It is armed with two M134 mini guns, an M230 30 mm chain gun, 70 mm Hydra rockets, and AGM-114 Hellfire air-to-ground missiles. A crew of four flies it.

The MH-47 Chinook is a large, dual-rotor helicopter built to deliver, extract, and resupply Special Operations Forces. It measures an impressive 99 feet (30.2 m) long. A family of MH-47 helicopters with different designations (MH-47E, MH-47G, etc.) is flown by the 160th Special Operations Aviation Regiment (SOAR). Chinook helicopters in this regiment can refuel other

The U.S. Army relies on swift, powerful MH-60 Black Hawk helicopters—shown in flight over Afghanistan—to provide armed escort and fire support for Special Operations Forces.

helicopters on the ground and deliver large payloads suspended from a sling below the helicopter.

In recent years, the MH-47 saw heavy use in the mountainous regions of Afghanistan. It has a maximum speed of 195 miles per hour (314 km/h) but cruises at 132 miles per hour (212 km/h). The MH-47 can fly 525 nautical miles (604 miles, or 972 km) before refueling. It is operated by a combat crew of six and carries M134 and M240 machine guns.

GETTING THERE: TROOP TRANSPORT ON THE GROUND

Marine Corps Special Forces are the front-line marines and sailors who provide special operations services in small teams. They are highly trained to operate in harsh situations where military objectives aren't always clear. Known as Critical Skills Operators (or Special Operators), they attend the Marine Corps Operations School to take part in a seven-month training program that includes direct action, close quarters battle, special reconnaissance, foreign internal defense, fire support, tactical casualty care, irregular warfare, survival evasion resistance and escape, and infantry weapons and tactics.

Once they land, Special Ops forces rely on many types of vehicles, from armed transports and six-wheel-drive trucks to motorcycles and all-terrain vehicles. In 1983, the High Mobility Multipurpose Wheeled Vehicle (HMMWV) was introduced to replace the M151-series jeep. The HMMWV—known to civilians as a Humvee—is a light tactical vehicle used for command and control, as a special purpose shelter carrier, and as a weapons platform on the battlefield. The Humvee found its way into the public eye after a strong showing in Operation Desert Storm (1991) and Operation Enduring Freedom (2001–2002). Civilian versions were even produced. Later military versions were built with armored panels, stronger engines, and even air conditioning. Over a thirty-year run, military Humvee vehicles aged and were retired, and the military moved to other transport vehicles.

Taking a drive through Afghanistan's Helmand Province? The Ground Mobility Vehicle (GMV), a heavily armored and upgraded Humvee, is your best choice.

LIFE AFTER HUMVEES

Today, Special Operations forces use a Ground Mobility Vehicle, or GMV, which is a modified Humvee. Different versions of GMVs are used by Special Forces, the 75th Ranger Regiment, Navy SEALs, and other teams. GMVs have been upgraded from the Humvee platform with a heavier suspension, more rugged tires, and a more powerful engine. They have higher ground clearance to drive above rocky terrain, an open bed for storing gear and supplies, a towing winch, and a Global Positioning System (GPS). GMVs are equipped with mounts for weapons such as M2 machine guns, M240 belt-fed machine guns, MK19 grenade launches, or the M249 SAW machine gun.

The U.S. Marine Corps and their Marine Special Operations Battalions have turned to the M1161 Internally Transportable-Light Strike Vehicle (ITV-LSV). This looks like an open-sided and extended jeep, with little protection from attack. The M1161 vehicle is built for light utility, light strike, and scout missions. It's designed to be transported aboard the MV-22 Osprey, a tilt-rotor aircraft that lands and takes off vertically, then flies like a conventional airplane.

The M1161 LSV is powered by a four-cylinder turbo-diesel engine. It is equipped with four-wheel steering and run-flat tires, inserts, and rims. Built for off-road use, the vehicle can carry enough gear and supplies for up to three days in the field. It has a top speed of about 65 miles per hour (105 km/h) on paved

CUP HOLDERS ARE INCLUDED

With all the rugged military vehicles available, why did the USSOCOM buy civilian versions of Toyota Tacoma pickup trucks for Special Operations Forces?

Answer: They needed nonstandard tactical vehicles (NSTVs) for use in Afghanistan and Iraq, often for covert operations. Unlike military-green vehicles that use clattery, noisy diesel engines, the Toyota trucks have quieter gasoline engines and drew less attention than traditional GMVs and LSVs. At the U.S. Army's Fort Campbell in Kentucky, the trucks were refitted with a machine gun mount, a roll bar, infrared lamps instead of regular headlights, antennas for military radio communications, and a winch. Technicians also removed and disconnected all the trucks' interior and exterior lights and warning chimes for nighttime duty. However, they kept the cup holders.

roads. Several armaments, such as the M240 machine gun, M2 heavy machine gun, and 40mm automatic grenade launcher can be mounted on the M1161.

OTHER LAND VEHICLES

While GMVs and LSVs are great in most situations, they are only two of the land vehicles that Special Ops troops use. Others include:

- The Desert Patrol Vehicle (DPV), a three-man, dune buggy–style vehicle. Navy SEALs and the Army's Delta Force have used the DPV in desert operations, long-range reconnaissance, and deep strike missions.

• The Ranger Special Operations Vehicle (SOV), a seven-passenger light-attack and reconnaissance vehicle based on the British-built Land Rover Defender. Smaller than a Humvee, it can be transported by Chinook helicopter.

• The Interim Fast Attack Vehicle (IFAV) operated by the U.S. Marine Corps' Force Recon unit. Three soldiers—a gunner, driver, and truck commander—crew the IFAV. The IFAV is a modified Mercedes Benz Wolf 290GDT 4x4 vehicle, resembling an open top SUV. Like the SOV, the IFAV can be carried by helicopter or MV-22 Osprey aircraft to its mission.

• The Pinzgauer SOV, used by Delta Force, is a six-wheel-drive, all-terrain vehicle with three wheels on each side. The Austrian-built Pinzgauer also has mounts for an M240 or M249 machine gun, M2 heavy machine gun, or MK19 grenade launcher.

ON AND IN THE WATER

Although Navy SEALs aren't confined to sea missions, they and other Special Operations Forces need flexible watercraft that are fast, versatile, and easy to transport. It's not unusual for Special Forces to use kayaks and canoes on covert operations. But powered watercraft are an essential part of the Special Ops fleet when missions call for insertion, extraction, and combat.

In the Middle East, U.S. Navy SEALs sometimes need to board oil platforms. This photo shows a Navy SEAL special boat team training with a Rigid-Hull Inflatable Boat (RHIB).

The Rigid-Hull Inflatable Boat (RHIB) is a high-performance combat boat used for short-range insertion and extraction of Special Ops forces. Powered by two diesel engines, RHIBs are also employed in limited coastal patrol, interdiction (disruption or destruction of enemy forces or supplies), and reconnaissance.

Heavy aircraft, including the C-5 Galaxy, C-17 Globemaster, and C-130 Hercules, can carry an RHIB. RHIBs can also be air-dropped from a C-130 or larger military aircraft. Each RHIB is 36 feet (11 m) long and is crewed by three special warfare combatant craft crewmen. The RHIB can carry eight SEALs. It has mounts for an M2HB machine gun, M240 machine gun, and MK19 grenade launcher.

The MK V Special Operations Craft (SOC) is a powerful twin-engine boat operated by a crew of five. It can carry up to sixteen Navy SEALs and their gear.

The vessel is most often used to insert and extract Navy SEALs or other U.S. Special Operations Forces from mission sites.

The MK V can also be used as a coastal patrol and reconnaissance vessel. It carries up to four Combat Rubber Raiding Craft (CRRC) and their outboard engines. A ramp at the stern enables CRRCs to quickly launch and return to the mother ship.

UAVs (unmanned aerial vehicles) can also be launched, operated, and recovered from an MK V. The 82-foot (25-m) MK V SOC has five mounts for machine guns and grenade launchers. It can reach speeds of up to 50 knots (57.5 miles per hour, or 92.6 km/h).

The MK8 MOD 1 SEAL Delivery Vehicle (SDV) is a free-flooding wet submersible—an open-cockpit underwater craft. It's engineered for undersea special operations including direct action, hydrographic reconnaissance, and insertion and extraction of Navy SEALs. SDVs can be inserted into the water via a DDS-equipped submarine, MK V SOC, or surface ship. The crew operates the vehicle while using underwater breathing gear, such as a Re-Breather, which also allows Special Forces soldiers to navigate rivers and streams undetected. Running on batteries, the SDV has its own propulsion, navigation, communication, and life-support systems.

Powered by a 55-horsepower engine, the CRRC is an inflatable "Zodiac" boat. Special Forces teams can carry them uninflated. CCRCs may be dropped by aircraft or larger boats, like the MK V SOC. Navy SEALS and other U.S. Special Operations units use

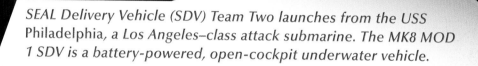

SEAL Delivery Vehicle (SDV) Team Two launches from the USS Philadelphia, a Los Angeles–class attack submarine. The MK8 MOD 1 SDV is a battery-powered, open-cockpit underwater vehicle.

the F470 model of the CRRC. It has multiple air chambers, which helps it stay afloat if one is punctured. On covert missions, CRRCs can be paddled to avoid detection. Once deployed with their SEAL teams, they can be inflated on the water's surface, using a foot pump or canister of CO_2. Up to six SEALs usually occupy a 15-foot (4.6-m) CRRC.

CHAPTER 6

ESSENTIALS: MRES, UNIFORMS, HELMETS, AND ARMOR

A long with weapons, explosives, and radio gear, food and water are the most essential items a Special Forces soldier can carry. What's the key difference between feeding Special Forces troops and regular army or navy servicemen? Special Forces teams aren't resupplied daily and must carry their packed food for longer missions.

These teams carry MREs—meals, ready to eat—that are packaged, stabilized, and sterilized to preserve them without refrigeration. Properly packaged, they can last up to five years without spoiling. For these reasons, civilians, scout troops, and other nonmilitary groups buy MREs in cartons for use on camping trips and survivalist encampments.

WHAT'S ON THE MRE MENU?

According to the U.S. Army, each MRE is one self-contained, nutritional meal. This includes a main course or entrée, such as spaghetti, tortilla, or beef stew; a starchy side dish like rice, corn, mashed potatoes, or fruit; peanut butter, jelly, or cheese spread with crackers or bread; cookies or pound cakes for dessert; candy items such as M&Ms, Skittles, or Tootsie Rolls; and a drink mix. Soldiers add water to the drink mixes to make beverages, including a Gatorade-like drink, cocoa, dairy shakes, coffee, and tea.

A modern MRE might consist of a chicken fajita, rice, chocolate pudding, baked snack crackers and a cheese spread, flavored coffee mix, a seasoning blend, a spoon, a flameless heater, and hot beverage bag. Flameless heaters let troops heat up their meals. The heaters are small pouches that contain a mix of iron, magnesium, and sodium. To use a flameless heater, soldiers simply add a little water. This causes a chemical reaction that produces heat. Soldiers warm up food by placing it in a bag with the heater for about twelve minutes.

An MRE provides an average of 1,250 calories, with enough protein, fat, and carbohydrates to fuel a soldier who'd be hiking over difficult terrain. One MRE contains one-third of the military recommended daily allowance of vitamins and minerals. Special Forces members are expected to consume three MREs per day.

Special Forces soldiers might be the ultimate "picky eaters." To reduce their loads as much as

The twenty-four MRE entrée options include several vegetarian selections. MREs were developed in 1980, replacing the MCI (Meal, Combat, Individual) rations that had been used in the 1960s and 1970s.

possible, they'll often take apart a supply of MREs, remove unneeded packaging, and repack them with only the foods they need and want to eat. By doing this, they can reduce the volume of food they carry by 60 percent and cut the weight of their MREs by half.

UNIFORMS FOR TODAY'S COMBAT

Each branch of the U.S. armed forces talks of the honor of "wearing the uniform." But Special Forces soldiers' day-to-day uniform differs dramatically from dress blues or the fatigues worn by yesterday's soldiers. Most often, the Special Forces soldier wears a BDU (battle dress uniform) with a "multicam" pattern. Multicam, short for multiple camouflage, is a design that helps soldiers blend in or hide in different environments and light conditions. There are several different multicam patterns. Some mix different shades of green, gray, and black on a darker green background. Units deployed in desert regions wear uniforms that feature patches of tan, beige, and black on a muted light brown fabric.

BUILT FOR TRAVEL

MREs must withstand parachute drops from 1,250 feet (381 m) and non-parachute drops of 100 feet (30.5 m). While MREs can last up to five years, the military packaging requirements say that they must have a minimum shelf life of three and a half years at 80 degrees F (26.7° C), or nine months at 100° F (37.8° C).

As Special Forces soldiers switched from metal canteens to flexible CamelBak or other wearable hydration bladders, "beverage bags" were added to the MRE in 2006. These bags make it easier to mix powdered drink mixes without a canteen's metal cup. Beverage bags include measuring marks to indicate levels of liquid for precise measurement. The bags can be sealed and placed inside the flameless heater.

Today's Special Forces soldiers rely on combat shirts, field shirts, and jackets that provide moisture-wicking and temperature-control materials. Troops can use insertable elbow pads for added comfort. All combat pants have ten pockets and allow soldiers to insert kneepads.

TODAY'S HIGH-TECH HELMETS

Today's Special Forces helmet must do more than protect a soldier's head and brain. To maximize their effectiveness, helmets are often fitted with night-vision devices, a light, and/or communications gear, freeing the soldier's hands for combat and weapons. Helmets currently in use include:

• The MICH 2000, a helmet developed for the Special Operations Forces Personal Equipment Advanced Requirements (SPEAR) program. MICH stands for Modular/Integrated Communications Helmet. This modular helmet system offers a soldier ballistic, fragmentation, hearing, and impact protection. The Kevlar-bonded helmet is compatible with night vision, communications, and nuclear, biological, and chemical

The helmet worn by this U.S. Army Ranger includes a mount for a camera, a flashlight, and a radio microphone to maintain contact with other troops.

equipment. AN/PVS-15 night-vision goggles may be mounted on the helmet, with the goggles' battery pack mounted on the back. The helmet also features a chemically powered headlight.

- The Protech Delta 4 Ballistic Helmet, chosen for Special Ops use for its extreme ballistic protection capability. The helmet's lightweight structure is another plus. This helmet allows mounting of night-vision goggles, a flashlight, and an infrared strobe.
- The Future Assault Shell Technology (FAST) helmet, used by soldiers in the U.S. Marines Special Operations Command.
- The HALO helmet, used in high altitude low opening (HALO) jumps made from extreme heights, which require an oxygen supply. Jumping from a high altitude allows entire Special Forces teams, undetected by radar, to infiltrate a combat area.

BODY ARMOR: EFFECTIVE, NOT BULLETPROOF

The first thing soldiers learn about body armor? It's not bulletproof. The second thing? The best body armor in the world will not help people who are not wearing it.

Body armor is designed to protect a soldier's chest and back. It usually includes plates to protect the groin and legs, too. The National Institute of Justice (NIJ) develops and tests body armor for use by the military and law enforcement. NIJ created standard classifications for body armor. Type I body armor offers the minimum level of protection. Type II-A armor protects against 9mm full-metal jacketed round-nose bullets, and so on. The highest level of protection comes from Type IV body armor, which protects against .30-caliber armor-piercing bullets.

Effective body armor emerged from the U.S. experience in the Vietnam War during the 1960s and 1970s. In that war, soldiers, marines, and airmen were issued flak vests that could stop shrapnel but not bullets. These early vests weren't comfortable. In the 1970s and 1980s, new materials, including Kevlar, ceramics, and ballistic nylon, helped lead to the development of practical body armor that could help protect soldiers from some gunfire.

Through the mid-2000s, the Personnel Armor System for Ground Troops (PASGT) vest was used widely by the U.S. military. It still sees some use today. PASGT consists of a front-opening vest and helmet. The vest protects a soldier's upper torso with a thirteen-layer ballistic filler of water-repellent Kevlar 29 fabric, covered with ballistic nylon cloth. The PASGT vest helps stop or slow down fragments from exploding munitions.

Today, an Improved Modular Tactical Vest (IMTV) used by the marines provides better protection and allows soldiers to move more easily. Soldiers can add or remove plates, pockets, and other add-ons as needed. The IMTV is more comfortable, distributes the combat load weight more efficiently, and makes it easier to handle a weapon. The standard IMTV offers front, side, and back protection against shrapnel and 9mm pistol rounds. For added protection against rifle rounds, enhanced small arms protective inserts called SAPI plates can be slipped inside the vest.

Army Rangers, U.S. Air Force, and other military units have adopted Releasable Body Armor Vests (RBAVs) that are more customizable. RBAVs are replacing the heavier Ranger Body Armor (RBA) once used by U.S. Army's 75th Ranger Regiment. The RBAV's quick-release features (using side-release buckles and Velcro) allow soldiers to remove the vest quickly during water accidents or when in need of rapid medical treatment. Depending on the need, RBAVs can accept soft or hard body armor plates of varying thickness. Soldiers can also add or detach sections to protect the collar, groin, and deltoid areas. These vests also include side pockets and slots for inserts, cable, magazines, radios, and other gear. As women begin to serve in Special Forces, the military is issuing body armor tailored with narrower shoulders and shorter torsos to fit female soldiers.

In the field, troops don't wear body armor all the time. It's cumbersome and heavy, especially along with the rest of their gear. So, they carry their armor plates—along with sensors, batteries, and tools—in a tactical plate carrier, which resembles an oversized "bucket boss" canvas tool carrier with shoulder straps. This has replaced some ballistic vests worn by troops. A soldier can add side armor, pelvic, groin, bicep, and deltoid protection, and even drop-leg ballistic panels. The plate carrier is a blend of military-spec nylon and DuPont Kevlar material that's lighter than standard tactical nylon—but ten times stronger.

HOW DOES BODY ARMOR WORK?

Body armor is designed to prevent a bullet or munitions fragment from penetrating a soldier's torso and damaging internal organs. In combat, two factors—the ballistic vest material and the armor plates—can prevent serious injury or death.

Bullets don't "bounce off" a body armor vest. Instead, the vest helps blunt the bullet's impact. For example, armor made of metal, reinforced plastic, or ceramic may be thick enough that it doesn't deform when struck by a bullet. If the armor does deform or crack, the bullet's impact may bruise the tissue under the armor. The internal organs may not be damaged, but if the impact and trauma are severe, contusions or internal injuries can occur.

When a bullet strikes body armor, a web of very strong fibers captures the bullet and absorbs and disperses its impact energy. The bullet may deform or flatten like a mushroom against the vest. Each layer of material in the vest helps dissipate the bullet's energy, ultimately slowing the bullet so it doesn't penetrate the skin.

Like the plate carrier, body armor is continually being improved. However, the process has not been without setbacks. In November 2012, ABC News reported that thousands of the newest ceramic body armor plates worn by U.S. Special Operations troops were recalled after the Department of Defense found defects in about 5 percent of the Generation III ballistic armor plates. While no one was killed or wounded as a result of the manufacturing defects, USSOCOM recalled the new plates and replaced them with Generation II plates until new armor was manufactured.

What's next? How about an Iron Man–like suit for Special Forces? In late 2013, Admiral William H. McRaven, head of USSOCOM, said he'd like to see an Iron Man suit for special operators. The suit would repel bullets and offer super-human strength. The

It's not a true "Iron Man" suit, but U.S. Army Sgt. Matthew Oliver's futuristic Tactical Assault Light Operator Suit concept drew plenty of attention at the 2012 Chicago Auto Show.

U.S. Army Research, Development and Engineering Command's official Twitter page stated the U.S. wanted a contract for an Iron Man suit in 2014, with full field testing to take place about four years afterward. SOCOM named the project Tactical Assault Light Operator Suit (TALOS) and asked several companies to come up with prototypes.

This is just one of many incredible weapons and gear the future holds for Special Operations soldiers— even without Stark Industries' participation. Today's armed forces consistently test and adopt new weapons and gear and gradually phase out existing hardware and equipment. If you want to learn about weapons in the testing stage or discover what gear was approved last week, check out the websites of the Special Ops branches. There are some fascinating weapons and gear under development!

GLOSSARY

BALLISTIC Having to do with projectiles, such as bullets.

CARBINE A short rifle, usually with a 13-to-16-inch (33-to-40-cm) barrel.

COUNTERINSURGENCY Military or political action taken against activities of guerrillas or rebels.

COUNTERTERRORISM Stopping terrorists before they strike by preventing formation of terrorist cells.

DIRECT ACTION Quick-strike missions to recover personnel or material or to seize, capture, or destroy a target.

FIRE SUPPORT Long-range firepower provided to a front-line military unit, often by artillery or close air support.

FOREIGN INTERNAL DEFENSE Training military forces in other countries to fight terrorists.

HUMANITARIAN SERVICE Providing aid and support to civilians as part of a military mission.

HYDROGRAPHIC RECONNAISSANCE Examining and charting of an area of water.

MAGAZINE A case that holds several rounds of bullets, enabling a soldier to fire repeatedly before reloading.

MORTAR A lightweight, compact weapon used to fire explosive charges at an enemy from a distance.

RADAR A device that sends out radio waves to determine the position and speed of an object.

SOUND SUPPRESSOR A device that, when attached to the barrel of a firearm, reduces noise and muzzle flash.

SPECIAL RECONNAISSANCE Going behind enemy lines undetected to gather intelligence.

STEALTH TECHNOLOGY Any technology or design that makes an aircraft hard to detect.

FOR MORE INFORMATION

Canadian War Museum
1 Vimy Place
Ottawa, ON K1A 0M8
Canada
(800) 555-5621
Website: http://www.warmuseum.ca
This museum showcases military armaments, vehicles, and other artifacts detailing Canada's armed forces engagements from the earliest times to today.

U.S. Air Force
1670 Air Force Pentagon
Washington, DC 20330-1670
Website: http://www.af.mil
The U.S. Air Force's mission today is "to fly, fight and win... in air, space and cyberspace."

U.S. Army
1500 Army Pentagon
Washington, DC 20310-1500
Website: http://www.army.mil
The army's mission is to fight and win wars by providing prompt, sustained land dominance across the full range of military operations and spectrum of conflict in support of combatant commanders.

U.S. Marine Corps
3000 Marine Corps Pentagon
Washington, DC 20350-3000
Website: http://www.marines.mil

The Marine Corps has approximately 154,000 troops and more than 18,000 officers.

U.S. Navy
1200 Navy Pentagon
Washington, DC 20350-1200
Website: http://www.navy.mil
The U.S. Navy defends U.S. interests with a fleet of some 290 vessels, including battleships, submarines, aircraft carriers, and support ships.

U.S. Special Operations Command (USSOCOM)
MacDill Air Force Base
7701 Tampa Point Boulevard
Tampa, FL 33621-5323
(813) 826-4600
Website: http://www.socom.mil
USSOCOM is based on a large U.S. Air Force installation on the edge of Tampa Bay. Special Forces missions throughout the world are planned and coordinated from USSOCOM's headquarters.

WEBSITES

Because of the changing nature of Internet links, Rosen Publishing has developed an online list of websites related to the subject of this book. This site is updated regularly. Please use this link to access the list:

http://www.rosenlinks.com/ISF/Weap

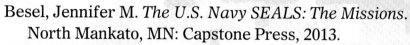

FOR FURTHER READING

Besel, Jennifer M. *The U.S. Navy SEALS: The Missions.* North Mankato, MN: Capstone Press, 2013.

Couch, Dick. *Chosen Soldier: The Making of a Special Forces Warrior.* New York, NY: Three Rivers Press, 2008.

Durant, Michael J., with Steven Hartov. *In the Company of Heroes.* New York, NY: Signet Publishing, 2006.

Gregory, Josh. *Special Ops.* North Mankato, MN: Cherry Lake Publishing, 2013.

McManners, Hugh. *Ultimate Special Forces.* New York, NY: Dorling Kindersley, 2003.

Montana, Jack. *Navy SEALs.* Broomall, PA: Mason Crest Publishers, 2011.

Neville, Leigh. *Special Operations Forces in Iraq.* New York, NY: Osprey Publishing, 2008.

Pushies, Fred. *MARSOC: U.S. Marine Corps Special Operations Command.* New York, NY: Zenith Press, 2011.

Robinson, Linda. *One Hundred Victories: Special Ops and the Future of American Warfare.* New York, NY: Public Affairs Publishing, 2013.

Schwalm, Tony. *The Guerrilla Factory: The Making of Special Forces Officers, the Green Berets.* New York, NY: Simon & Schuster, 2013

Telep, Peter. *Direct Action: Special Forces Afghanistan.* New York, NY: Berkley Publishing Group, 2008.

United States Special Operations Command. *U.S. Special Operations Command Fact Book: 2014.* MacDill Air Force Base, FL: USSOCOM Public Affairs, 2014.

BIBLIOGRAPHY

AmericanSpecialOps.com. "M240 Machine Gun." Retrieved March 3, 2014. (http://www.americanspecialops.com/special-ops-weapons/m240.php).

Army Study Guide. "M4 Carbine." Quinn Street Inc. Retrieved March 8, 2014. (http://www.armystudyguide.com/content/army_board_study_guide_topics/m4/m4-carbine.shtml).

GlobalSecurity.org. "Body Armor." Retrieved March 6, 2014 (http://www.globalsecurity.org/military/systems/ground/body-armor.htm).

Harris Corporation. "Tactical Communications Products and Systems." Retrieved March 12, 2014 (http://rf.harris.com/products/default.asp).

Hoffman, Mike. "Momentum Builds for Iron Man Suit." Military.com, December 31, 2013. Retrieved March 5, 2014 (http://kitup.military.com/2013/12/momentum-builds-iron-man-suit.html#more-27205).

Ingersoll, Geoffrey, and Robert Johnson. "18 Things Navy SEALs Won't Leave Home Without." BusinessInsider.com, September 13, 2012. Retrieved March 9, 2014. (http://www.businessinsider.com/these-are-18-things-navy-seals-are-probably-taking-with-them-to-libya-right-now-2012-9?op=1).

Johnson, Steve. "SEALs upgrade to SIG Sauer P226 Mk25 Pistol." TheFirearmsBlog.com, November 17, 2011. Retrieved March 1, 2014 (http://www.thefirearmblog.com/blog/2011/11/17/seals-upgrade-to-sig-sauer-p226-mk25-pistol).

Kapacziewski, Joseph, and Charles W. Sasser. *Back in the Fight: The Explosive Memoir of a Special Operator Who Never Gave Up.* New York, NY: St. Martin's Press, 2013.

Lopez, C. Todd. "New first aid kit includes eye protection, strap cutter." U.S. Army, December 6, 2013. Retrieved March 6, 2014 (http://www.army.mil/article/116565/New_ first_aid_kit_includes_eye_protection__strap_cutter).

Military.com. "Marine Corps Special Forces (MARSOC) Training." Retrieved March 1, 2014 (http://www .military.com/special-operations/marine-corps-marsoc -training.html).

Neville, Leigh. *Special Operations Forces in Afghanistan.* New York, NY: Osprey Publishing, 2008.

Newcomb, Alyssa. "Special Ops Body Armor Recalled After Safety Defects Found." *ABC News*, November 24, 2012. Retrieved March 1, 2014 (http://abcnews.go.com/US/ special-ops-body-armor-recalled-safety-defects-found/ story?id=17800154).

O'Toole, Molly. "Women in Combat May Be Able to Train for Special Forces Roles." *Huffington Post*, June 18, 2013. Retrieved March 7, 2014 (http://www.huffingtonpost .com/ 2013/06/18/women-in-combat-special-ops_n_ 3461065.html).

Owen, Mark, with Kevin Maurer. *No Easy Day: The Autobi- ography of a Navy SEAL.* New York, NY: Dutton, 2012.

Sodaro, Craig. *The U.S. Marines Special Operations Regi- ment: The Missions.* North Mankato, MN: Capstone Press, 2012.

U.S. Army. "Meals, Ready to Eat." Retrieved March 13, 2014 (http://www.goarmy.com/soldier-life/fitness-and-nutrition/ components-of-nutrition/meals-ready-to-eat.html).

U.S. Army. "Special Forces: Equipment." Retrieved March 5, 2014 (http://www.goarmy.com/special-forces/ equipment.html).

U.S. Army. "Special Forces: Helicopters." Retrieved March 6, 2014 (http://www.goarmy.com/special-forces/ helicopters.html).

INDEX

ABOUT THE AUTHOR

David Kassnoff is a communications professional, writer, and educator who has worked with veterans' organizations and has more than twenty years' experience with professionals and executives in corporate and not-for-profit organizations. His writing has appeared in many mainstream and industry publications, including *American Biotechnology Laboratory*, *Diversity Executive*, *Profiles in Diversity Journal*, *USA Weekend*, *Audio-Visual Communications*, the Gannett Rochester Newspapers, *Photo Marketing*, *Rochester Business* magazine, the *Los Angeles Times* magazine, *Photo Trade News*, and *Practical Homeowner*. He also serves as an adjunct professor in the Russell J. Jandoli School of Journalism and Mass Communication at St. Bonaventure University. His work has been recognized for excellence by the New York State Newspaper Publishers Association and the Council for Advancement and Support of Education.

PHOTO CREDITS

Cover inset photos far left U.S. Air Force, center left and far right www.army.mil, center right U.S. Marine Corps/Lance Cpl. Ashton Buckingham; cover background (flare) © iStockphoto.com/Evgeny Terentev; cover background (smoke) © iStockphoto.com/Antagain; cover background and interior (crosshairs) © iStockphoto.com/marlanu; p. 5 U.S. Army; p. 8 Scott Nelson/Getty Images; p. 11 DoD photo/SFC Silas Toney; pp. 13, 16 © AP Images; p. 18 U.S. Air Force/Master Sgt. Cohen A. Young; p. 20 DefenseImagery.mil/Cpl. Eric R. Martin/U.S. Marine Corps; p. 23 DefenseImagery.mil/SRA Joshua Strang/U.S. Air Force; p. 24 DefenseImagery.mil/Sgt. Mallory S. VanderSchans/U.S. Marine Corps; pp. 28–29 U.S. Navy/James Woods; p. 33 U.S. Navy/MCS Seaman Sheldon Rowley; p. 36 U.S. Navy/PO1 Matthew Leistikow; p. 38 www.army.mil/Spc. David Gunn; p. 42 U.S. Navy/MCS3 Class Adam Henderson/Released; p. 44 U.S. Navy/CPhoM Andrew McKaskle; p. 47 U.S. Marine Corps; p. 49 © Stocktrek Images, Inc./Alamy; p. 54 U.S. Army; interior graphics © iStockphoto.com/P_Wei (camouflage), © iStockphoto.com/Oleg Zabielin (silhouette), © iStockphoto.com/gary milner (texture).

Designer: Brian Garvey; Editor: Jeanne Nagle